Editor
Eric Migliaccio

Managing Editor
Ina Massler Levin, M.A.

Illustrator
Vicki Frazier

Cover Artist
Barb Lorseyedi

Art Manager
Kevin Barnes

Art Director
CJae Froshay

Imaging
Craig Gunnell

Publisher
Mary D. Smith, M.S. Ed.

OCTOBER
DAILY JOURNAL
WRITING PROMPTS

Author

Maria Elvira Gallardo, M.A.

Teacher Created Resources, Inc.
6421 Industry Way
Westminster, CA 92683
www.teachercreated.com

ISBN: 978-1-4206-3127-2

©2005 Teacher Created Resources, Inc.
Reprinted, 2007
Made in U.S.A.

Table of Contents

Introduction

More than ever, it is important for students to practice writing on a daily basis. Every classroom teacher knows that the key to getting students excited about writing is introducing interesting topics that are fun to write about. *October Daily Journal Writing Prompts* provides kindergarten through second grade teachers with an entire month of ready-to-use journal topics, including special holiday and seasonal topics for October. All journal topics are included in a calendar that is easily reproduced for students. A student journal cover allows students to personalize their journal for the month.

Other useful pages that are fun include:

✣ **A Blank Calendar (pages 6 and 7)**
This can be used to meet your own classroom needs. You may want your students to come up with their own topics for the month, or it may come in handy for homework writing topics.

✣ **Word Banks (pages 40–43)**
These include commonly-used vocabulary words for school, holiday, and seasonal topics. A blank word bank gives students a place to write other words they have learned throughout the month.

✣ **October Author Birthdays (page 44)**
Celebrate famous authors' birthdays or introduce an author who is new to your students. This page includes the author's birthdays and titles of some of their most popular books.

✣ **October Historic Events (page 45)**
In the format of a timeline, this page is a great reference tool for students. They will love seeing amazing events that happened in October.

✣ **October Discoveries & Inventions (page 46)**
Kindle students' curiosity about discoveries and inventions with this page. This is perfect to use for your science and social studies classes.

Motivate your students' writing by reproducing the pages in this book and making each student an individual journal. Use all the journal topics included, or pick and choose them as you please. See "Binding Ideas" on page 48 for ways to put it all together. Planning a month of writing will never be easier!

O C T

1 I'm excited it's October because…	**2** My parents tell me never to…	**3** The best gift I ever received was…	**4** My favorite book is…
9 For Halloween I want to dress up as…	**10** I could prevent fires by…	**11** Children should be allowed to…	**12** A person I admire is…
17 Something I do with my family is…	**18** I get scared when…	**19** At home I have to…	**20** I like when our teacher…
25 I have always wondered…	**26** If I were sixteen…	**27** The nicest thing anyone has done for me is…	**28** I don't like it when people…

O B E R

5	6	7	8
A job I never want is…	A television show I always watch is…	I wish I could…	When I graduate high school…

13	14	15	16
During a fire drill…	My favorite sport is…	My friends like it when I…	I wish I could give my parents…

21	22	23	24
The last movie I saw was…	When I was a baby…	I like shopping for…	If I were a cartoon character, I would…

29	30	31	Special Topic
I love eating…	I'm proud of…	On Halloween my friends and I…	**Autumn** During autumn, I enjoy…

O C T

1	2	3	4
9	10	11	12
17	18	19	20
25	26	27	28

O B E R

5	6	7	8
13	14	15	16
21	22	23	24
29	30	31	Special Topic

I'm excited it's October because _____

_____

_____

_____

_____

_____

_____

_____

_____

My parents tell me never to _____

_____

_____

_____

_____

_____

_____

_____

_____

The best gift I ever received was _____

_____

_____

_____

_____

_____

_____

_____

_____

My favorite book is _____

_____

_____

_____

_____

_____

_____

_____

_____

_____

A job I never want is _____

_____

_____

_____

_____

_____

_____

_____

_____

A television show I always watch is _____

_____

_____

_____

_____

_____

_____

_____

I wish I could _____

_____

_____

_____

_____

_____

_____

                              _____

                              _____

                              _____

When I graduate high school _____

_____

_____

_____

_____

_____

_____

_____

_____

For Halloween I want to dress up as _____

_____

_____

_____

_____

_____

_____

                                        _____

                                        _____

                                        _____

I could prevent fires by _____

_____

_____

_____

_____

_____

_____

_____

Children should be allowed to _____

_____

_____

_____

_____

_____

_____

_____

_____

A person I admire is _____

_____

_____

_____

_____

_____

_____

_____

During a fire drill _____

_____

_____

_____

_____

_____

_____

_____

_____

_____

My favorite sport is _____

_____

_____

_____

_____

_____

_____

_____

_____

My friends like it when I _____

_____

_____

_____

_____

_____

_____

_____

_____

_____

I wish I could give my parents _____

_____

_____

_____

_____

_____

_____

_____

_____

Something I do with my family is _____

_____

_____

_____

_____

_____

_____

_____

24

I get scared when _____

_____

_____

_____

_____

_____

_____

_____

_____

At home I have to _____

_____

_____

_____

_____

_____

_____

_____

_____

_____

I like when our teacher _____

_____

_____

_____

_____

_____

_____

_____

$5 + 5 + 2 = 12$

_____

_____

The last movie I saw was _____

_____

_____

_____

_____

_____

_____

Now playing

Space Race

_____

_____

_____

When I was a baby _____
_____
_____
_____
_____
_____
_____
_____
_____

I like shopping for _____

_____

_____

_____

_____

_____

_____

_____

_____

_____

If I were a cartoon character, I would _____

_____

_____

_____

_____

_____

_____

_____

_____

I have always wondered _____

_____

_____

_____

_____

_____

_____

Interesting Facts

_____

_____

If I were sixteen _____

_____

_____

_____

_____

_____

_____

_____

_____

The nicest thing anyone has done for me is _____

_____

_____

_____

_____

_____

_____

_____

_____

I don't like it when people _____

_____

_____

_____

_____

_____

_____

_____

_____

I love eating _____

_____

_____

_____

_____

_____

_____

_____

_____

_____

I'm proud of _____

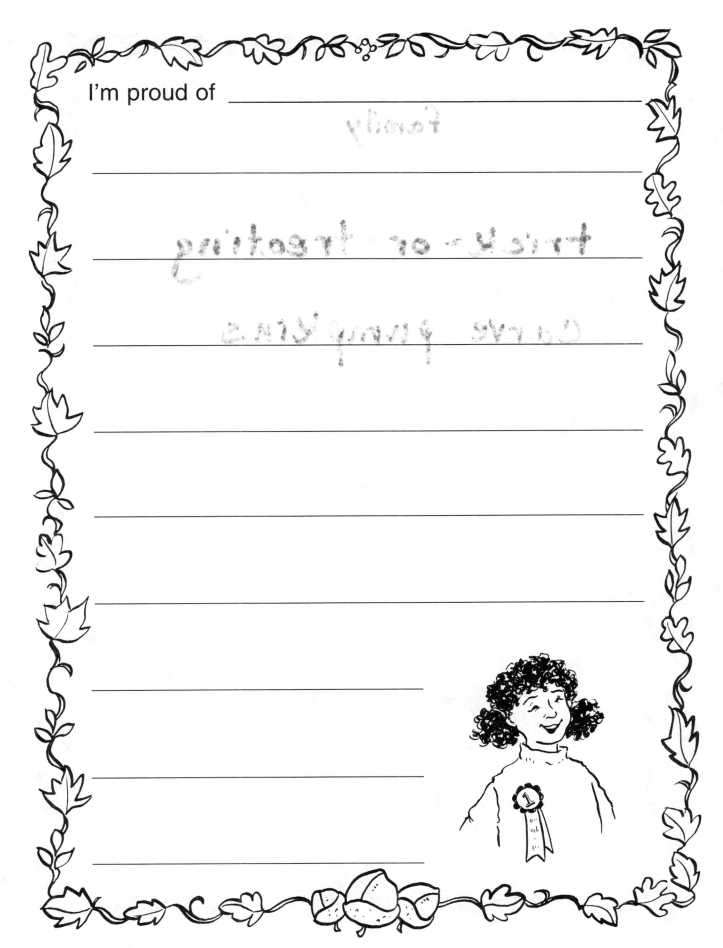

On Halloween my friends and I _____
family

_____

trick - or - treating

carve pumpkins

_____

_____

_____

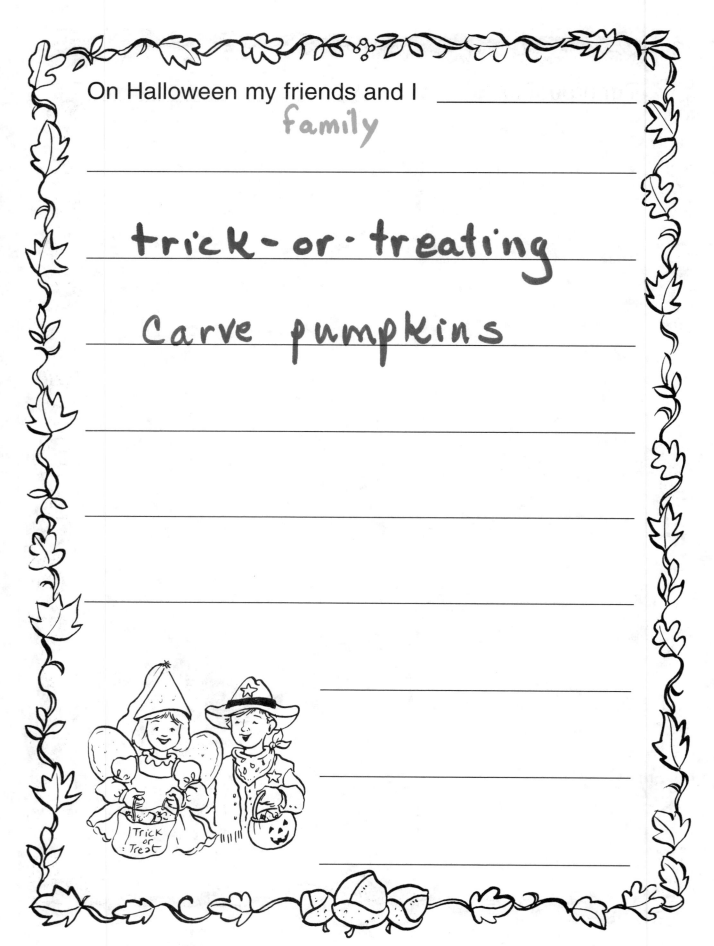

_____

_____

_____

During autumn, I enjoy _____

_____

_____

_____

_____

_____

_____

_____

_____

School Word Bank

activity	desks	map	recess
art	dictionary	markers	report
assembly	flag	math	ruler
award	games	music	science
backpack	glue	office	scissors
board	grades	paper	spelling
books	history	pencils	students
calendar	homework	pens	subject
classroom	learn	playground	teacher
computer	library	principal	test
crayons	lunch	reading	write

Holiday Word Bank

October Holidays

Canada's Thanksgiving Day	Columbus Day
Fire Protection Week	Halloween

alarm	fire escape	pumpkin
black	firefighter	safety
burn	ghost	*Santa Maria*
candy	land	scarecrow
celebration	maple syrup	ships
costume	mask	smoke
dinner	Newfoundland	Spain
discover	New World	spooky
emergency	*Niña*	trick-or-treat
explorer	orange	turkey
extinguisher	*Pinta*	voyage
family	prevent	wild rice

Seasonal Word Bank

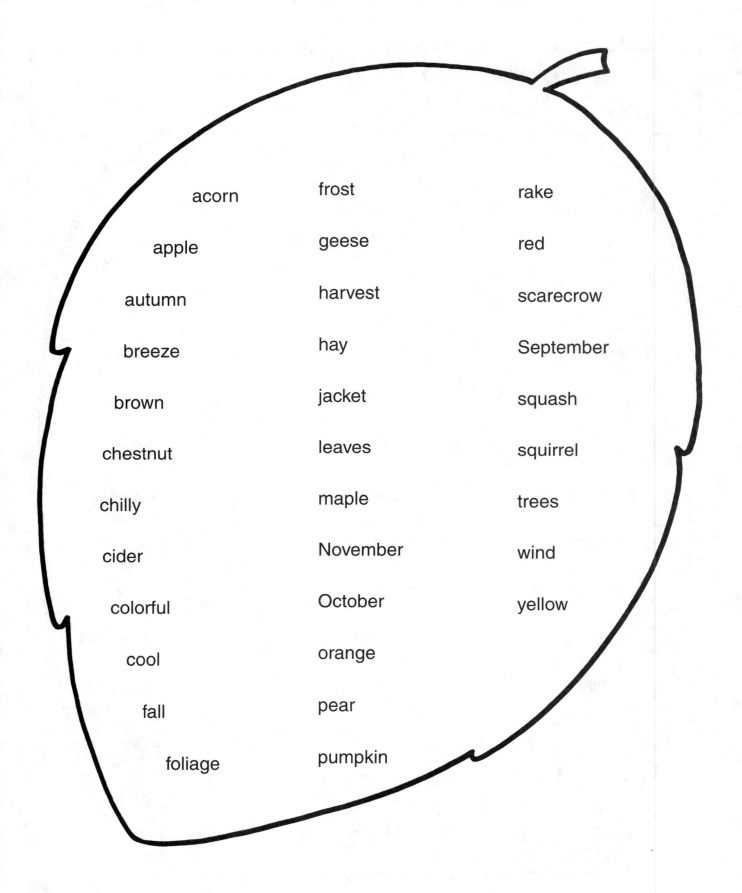

acorn	frost	rake
apple	geese	red
autumn	harvest	scarecrow
breeze	hay	September
brown	jacket	squash
chestnut	leaves	squirrel
chilly	maple	trees
cider	November	wind
colorful	October	yellow
cool	orange	
fall	pear	
foliage	pumpkin	

My Word Bank

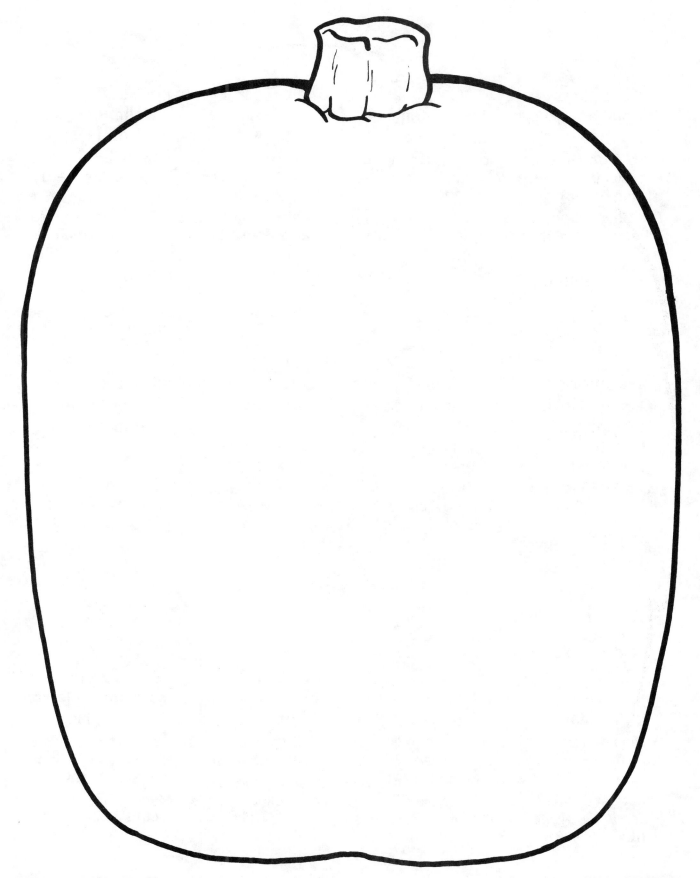

October Author Birthdays

1

Deborah Hautzig
(b. 1956)

Happy Birthday, Little Witch (Random House Inc., 1985)

The Secret Garden (Penguin, 1995)

3

Marilyn Singer
(b. 1948)

Good Day, Good Night (Marshall Cavendish, 1998)

Quiet Night (Clarion, 2002)

4

Susan Meddaugh
(b. 1944)

Martha Speaks (A Walter Lorraine Book, 1992)

Lulu's Hat (A Walter Lorraine Book, 2002)

8

Faith Ringgold
(b. 1930)

Tar Beach (Crown Publishers, 1991)

If A Bus Could Talk: The Story of Rosa Parks (Simon & Schuster, 1999)

9

Johanna Hurwitz
(b. 1937)

Class Clown (Morrow Junior, 1986)

Teacher's Pet (Morrow Junior, 1988)

Class President (Morrow Junior, 1990)

10

Nancy L. Carlson
(b. 1953)

I Like Me! (Viking Press, 1988)

ABC I Like Me! (Viking Children's Books, 1997)

14

Elisa Kleven
(b. 1958)

Hooray, A Piñata! (Dutton, 1996)

The Paper Princess Finds Her Way (Dutton, 2003)

19

Dan Gutman
(b. 1955)

The Kid Who Became President (Scholastic, 1999)

Miss Daisy Is Crazy! (HarperCollins, 2004)

21

Ann Cameron
(b. 1943)

Julian's Glorious Summer (Random House, 1989)

The Most Beautiful Place in the World (Knopf, 1998)

26

Steven Kellogg
(b. 1941)

Jack and the Beanstalk (William Morrow, 1991)

The Three Sillies (Candlewick Press, 1999)

30

Eric A. Kimmel
(b. 1946)

The Gingerbread Man (Holiday House, 1993)

Anasi and the Magic Stick (Holiday House, 2001)

31

Katherine Paterson
(b. 1932)

The Angel and the Donkey (Clarion Books, 1996)

Marvin One Too Many (HarperCollins, 2001)

October   Historic   Events

October 1, 1890

Yosemite National Park was established by United States Congress.

October 2, 1950

The comic strip *Peanuts* by Charles M. Schulz first published in seven U.S. newspapers.

October 6, 1927

The Jazz Singer, the first full-length "talking" movie, was released.

October 12, 1792

The first celebration of Columbus Day in the USA held in New York.

October 14, 1926

The children's book *Winnie-the-Pooh* by A.A. Milne was first published.

October 16, 1758

Dictionary Day celebrates Noah Webster's birthday. He compiled *Webster's Dictionary*.

October 16, 1893

Two school teachers, Mildred and Patty Smith Hill, copyrighted the words to the song "Happy Birthday to You."

October 25, 1886

The artist Pablo Picasso was born on this day in Malaga, Spain.

October 27, 1904

The New York City subway began operation.

October 28, 1886

The Statue of Liberty was dedicated by U.S. President Grover Cleveland in New York Harbor.

October 31, 1864

Nevada was admitted as the 36th U.S. state.

October
Discoveries & Inventions

1

People's Republic of China was founded on this day in 1949.

The first CD player (developed by Sony, Philips, and Polygram) went on sale for $625 in 1982. It was invented by physicist James T. Russell.

9

Mission Delores, the oldest building in San Francisco, CA, was founded in 1776.

11

A patent for the Comptometer, which was the first adding machine known to be absolutely accurate at all times, was issued on this day in 1887 to Dorr Eugene Felt

12

Bahamas Discovery Day commemorates the landing of Columbus in the Bahamas in 1492.

20

First "Internet" connection made in 1969. The first connection on what was to become the Internet was made between computers at UCLA and the Stanford Research Institute.

21

First incandescent lamp demonstrated by Thomas Edison in 1879. It burned for 13-and-a-half hours and was the first lamp that was economical enough to be used in homes.

22

First photocopy of a document was made in Astoria, New York, by Chester Carlson and Otto Kornei in 1938. They copied a slide that read "10-22-38 Astoria."

25

The first microwave oven designed for home use was unveiled by the Tappan Company in Mansfield, Ohio, in 1955. It was invented by Percy Spencer in 1945.

29

First ballpoint pen was sold at Gimbel's Department Store in New York in 1945. 10,000 Reynolds Rocket ballpoint pens were sold for $12.50 each. American inventor Milton Reynolds is credited as the inventor, although the real creators may actually have been two brothers from Argentina named Laszlo and Georg Biro.

October
Journal

by

_____

Binding Ideas

Students will be so delighted when they see a month of their writing come together with one of the following binding ideas. You may choose to bind their journals at the beginning or end of the month, once they have already filled all of the journal topic pages. When ready to bind students' journals, have them color in their journal cover on page 47. It may be a good idea to reproduce the journal covers on hard stock paper in order to better protect the pages in the journal. Use the same hard stock paper for the back cover.

Simple Book Binding

1. Put all pages in order and staple together along the left margin.

2. Cut book-binding tape to the exact length of the book.

3. Run the center line of tape along the left side of the book and fold to cover the front left margin and the back right margin. Your book is complete!

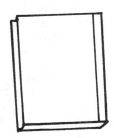

Yarn-Sewn Binding

1. Put all pages in order and hole-punch the left margin.

2. Stitch the pages together with thick yarn or ribbon.